Every Love Story Is an Apocalypse Story

Sundress Publications • Knoxville, TN

Copyright © 2016 by Donna Vorreyer
ISBN: 978-1-939675-27-9
Published by Sundress Publications
Editor: Sara Henning
http://www.sundresspublications.com

Colophon: This book is set in Bell MT.
Cover Design: Hannah Berling
Cover Image: "On the Horizon" by Brooke Shaden (www.brookeshaden.com)

Book Design: Sara Henning
Special Thanks: Erin Elizabeth Smith, Jane Huffman, T.A. Noonan

Every Love Story Is an Apocalypse Story
Donna Vorreyer

Thank Yous

Many of these poems were completed during a 2013 residency at Kimmel-Harding-Nelson Center for the Arts in Nebraska City, NE. I am grateful for their support.

Thank you to the Sundress family, especially Erin Elizabeth Smith and Sara Henning. My gratitude also goes out to Kristin LaTour, an incredible friend and first reader.

To my colleagues at Hinsdale Middle School who support my writing life. All of you who have talked to me about my work, attended readings, etc., make me grateful and proud to know you.

And, always, for Jeff—my guide through every little apocalypse.

TABLE OF CONTENTS

Preamble   9

Part One: No Quick Misery

I Swear I Am Not Your Ahab	13
Attraction of Opposites	14
Bringing in the Sheaves	15
I Put False Hope in Celestial Bodies	16
Curing the Distance	17
The Wind Lulled and It Commenced Raining*	18
Split	19
Traveling Draws the Veil	20
Surviving a Midwestern Winter	21
Compline with Folded Arms	22
This Was the Summer	23
We Set Sail Under a Gentle Breeze*	24
A Curse of Surfaces	25
Before and After*	26
It Started with the Apple Tree	28
Strut and Fret	29
In the Night Cathedral	31
How to Explain Emptiness	32

Part Two: There Has Been Damage

First Night Alone*	35
A Litany of Sorrows	36
Feral	37
Losing Ground	38
Therianthropy	39
Self-Portrait as Naturalist	40
Provisions	41
2 AM, Waning	42
After the Fires	44
I Remember You Best	45
Logging the Loss	46
What I Do in August	47
Lost Birds	48
Alphabet of Indecision	49
I Dream of Waking*	51

Matins with Horses and Light   52
A Case for Gravity   53
Trigger   54

Part Three: We Feast on This Believing

Day One Again   57
In the Garden   58
Since Nightmares are a Kind of Dreaming   59
Salvaging   60
Starting Over   61
Finally, An Understanding of Scale   62
This Being the Usual Signal*   63
We are painting the bedroom   64
Back to the Music   65
Continuing   66

Redux   67

Acknowledgments   69
About the Author   71

As far as love is concerned, possession, power, fusion and disenchantment are the Four Horsemen of the Apocalypse.
—Zygmunt Bauman

Preamble

When we meet, you notice
something in the air—lilacs
or lullabies, a subtle change
in the horizon's line.

This is desire when it's new.

We bind ourselves with cloth
and promises, leather bands
that tether us wrist to wrist,
knots wetted against unraveling.

We say they can't be broken.

We know this is a lie, know
that every paired or melded
thing returns to pieces. Still
we tremble, never sated.

We feast on this believing.

Part One: No Quick Misery

I Swear I Am Not Your Ahab

I will carve the one blue rib
from your chest
and paint a morning,
hoist one bleached sail
from your breath
and call it cloud.

I will scrub one black stain
from your skin
and tar the evening,
pluck one fine hair
from your neck
and call it mast.

I will break one dry bone
from your limbs
and row a midnight whirlpool,
trace one white promise
on your lips
and call it whale.

The Attraction of Opposites

That night, mist gathered warm around
our young heads, a tandem crown of smoke.
We watched lizards climb the terrace wall,

silvery feet skittering out of reach.
Down below, a siren howled warning as you
dropped the needle on some old forty-fives.

Blue tones tangled us in a wistful web.
Despite the softness of the notes, the night,
the roll of the waves, my skirt's flick and flow,

you were all ticks and angles, pacing hard
and peeling the sunburned skin from your
nose until I kissed you into curves. Even then,

you wanted us to be exact, defined, but we
would never be so. We are balls of mercury,
the sudden flame on the head of a match.

Bringing in the Sheaves

You chase me through a cornfield
and we arrive in a clearing. All
that we know and do not know
shimmers between us, an invisible
door with no way to open or close.

You can only stare at the horizon.
Hidden in the stalks, crickets sing.
I rub my thighs together in bold
commiseration. A thousand ears
listen for answers that do not come.

I do not know what you want, so I tear
at tassels, braid the pulled silk
into a gown the color of your hair.
You shrug, turn and motion for me
to follow you back to where we were.

I cannot find my way through,
so I run in the other direction, gown
streaming above my head, a banner.
All that is left is my rustle, a black confetti
of crickets littering the sky in my wake.

I Put False Hope in Celestial Bodies

Your orbits are erratic, strange parabolas of leaving
and returning, vast galaxies of lapis and ashes.

There is the promise of communication, but I have not
seen it—no flares, no comet tails, no meteor showers.

Light years away, you crush the moon to craters,
then draw close but never touch me. I wish I could say

you were the sun I revolve around, gathering warmth
with each rotation. Instead you are only some alien

shimmer in Orion's belt, not of this world or that one,
depositing your dust then disappearing. Still, I map

out constellations, look for patterns in the atmosphere.
I connect each black hole breath, each five-pointed scar.

Curing the Distance

I visit the priestess, but even her gimmicks
with chickens do not come through. I am still
a crash cart regular, though each sign is vital.

My bones sustain my frame despite rifts
and stutters. Your absence sets me on a flight
plan toward a cliff with two rickety wings.

I am a sad machine with broken levers, stripped
of speech and all sense. I try liquor to hypnotize,
drugs to numb the flesh. I fall asleep on trains.

So many miles between us, the threads all
unraveling. Give me a language for this
ache. Let the healing begin.

The Wind Lulled and It Commenced Raining

We were glad for
we had prayed
for rain,
for reason to huddle inside,
for shelter.
These little solaces
of moans and sighs,
this cabin witness.

Lust the best tonic
for forgetting: hard
boards, hard bed.
We lost ourselves beyond
logic as branches scraped
the walls and kept watch
while we wrestled
and bucked inside.

When the rain stopped,
you carved our initials
into the logs. Territorial
markings. I rubbed
my neck, bruises just
beneath the skin—badges
of our savage longing.

Split

We hobble lopsided, one rooted, one wandering.
I ask if you've forgotten how to loose your grip,
how to roam, untethered and wild. You ask if I recall
the certainty of stillness, the way muscles remember
their way through landscapes, even in darkness.

As nothing will unroot you, I will praise instead
how firm you stand as I test your will with wind,
tempt you with music, spices from far-off lands.
You will not go, stuck fast where you are planted,
content with rings of years, your vast canopy of sky.

Traveling Draws the Veil

Language is useless now. A mute shroud
has covered me, dragging a train of clouds.

I must change the names for everything:
the sunlight, a length of yellow string;

dawn, the fire of heaven, blood-red and quick
as a dagger. New blooms? Buttons. This sick

wild flutter of white plaster? Butterflies.
Wide church columns become giant cacti

in a desert city. Round-slung hammocks
harden to tortoise shells. Discarded blocks

of lumber curl, slither into serpents
which arc cursive over the hotel fence.

My tongue, a slab of sculptor's stone, my heart
a rough-carved anchor—such primitive art.

Surviving a Midwestern Winter

When you are bored with windows
and eight kinds of anger, each with
its own knotted scarf, each flustered
remedy a skinny dip in a frozen sea,

hide in the basement, revel in
summer honey, jarred and labeled
on a makeshift shelf, rows of small
suns whose amber glass must suffice.

Compline with Folded Arms

No sounds but a sitcom laugh track
and dogs scratching at their collars.
An observer might guess content,
but the familiar deceives. Face to face,

offenses branded on our foreheads
have already faded, but consequences
undulate in air, a current. There has
been damage, collateral and invisible.

Hurt is a live wire that passes between us,
powder burns on both our temples.
We wear the stoic stares of the battle-
worn. Our bodies do not touch.

This Was the Summer

of the sea pulling into itself, the science of tides,
the beach where we built castles and coffins

of lush orchards, trees fruit-laden and swaying, of initials
carved into unblemished bark, hands itching to peel it back

of infection, of the septic fester of broken oaths, the long con
of your Shawshank patience, waiting out my endless no

of regret, of me turning to the river, a shrouded thing,
hiding from day until I caught a sudden flashing, silver and liquid

of forgotten joy swimming upstream to greet me,
of losing, of learning there could be so much more to lose

We Set Sail Under a Gentle Breeze

Suddenly, the wind
turns. A sky that has been dark
dims to white.

We run to shore, discover
a skiff with oars bent outward
like welcoming arms.

Tadpoles skitter beneath
the bow as we balance
our weight then push off.

Loose-limbed, we row
the easy current, dip
into ripples, our day long,

the hours unticked by clocks.
Recall the sermons about sloth—
this is how ruin begins.

A Curse of Surfaces

Like Midas in reverse,
I tarnish everything I touch,
dull the luster of flowers
as I pluck them for a vase.

I discolor, disappoint.

The oils in my hands
season the wooden
banisters black. I dim
your face to frowns,

conceal, corrode,

each encounter
an experiment in patina.
I fumble on, staining
all my days.

Before and After

His arms were:
        bow and quiver
        green boughs
        and
        the skin of antelopes
        red willow
        a piece of fresh salmon
        roasted
        a bridle bit
        little patches of red cloth
        some flint
        some instruments
        of bone.

I discovered:
        his fierce eyes
        (a few indifferent knives)
        and his lank jaws
        (two brass kettles)
        in the same
        steadfast posture
        in the sweet
        scented grass
        with another.

All my hope transformed:
        quills of a porcupine
        falling timber
        old tin canisters
        filled with
        choke cherry
        and
        six small pieces
        of shell
        resembling pearl.

How to Explain This Emptiness

An overpass, deserted, looming over dust and yellow
wildflowers latticed by dirt.

A freight train snaking in the distance, all tankers,
fluids bound and bordered by rust.

A dilapidated church, its crossbeams split open,
releasing an undulate parabola of swallows.

The holy in what is not whole, the music in the
silence, another life thrown into this thresher.

The harsh twang of steel guitar like a death cry, like
a baby's wail. An unsteady hand suturing the wound.

Part Two: There Has Been Damage

First Night Alone

Dusk cracks its mandible,
shows its purpled mouth,
a hint of its waiting cavern.

Darkness stalks the tall grass,
a lone, furred dingo ready
to howl and start the hunt.

I am accustomed to being
twinned, a two-legged thing.
Unhinged, I lean toward falling.

Night pokes its muzzle to nudge
the door ajar. It licks my jaw,
its pink tongue a promise of dawn.

A Litany of Sorrows

Of soldiers and their sorrows,
their field packs strung
with photos of loved ones,
lovers who wait at home.

Of lovers and their sorrows,
days fraught with friction
and awkward admonitions
mouths can't seem to hold.

Of mouths and their sorrows,
angry tissue and tender teeth,
the rough-bitten inner cheeks
that nip back words like no.

Of words and their sorrows,
inadequate or fumbling, falling
from lips like stumbling
drunks, litanies of false hope.

Of litanies and their sorrows,
lines that repetitively plod
like prayers to a deafened god.
I cannot pretend to know

of gods and their sorrows
and so it ends. Amen. Amen.

Feral

Set fire to the chairs and run
to the woods, to the secret
hill where the ground is littered
with the black wings of crows.

Drape the fabric of your cloak
loose enough to let winter season
your blood. After a day, leave it
draped over a stone.

Let lights on a porch become
a memory. See your sister's head
for an instant at the window and
think only food.

Circle the wooded world as
visitor, never leaving a trace.
Be wary: there will be shots
as you prowl near a house,

days when your stomach is
an empty pocket, your tongue
hungry for the slightest scrap
or drip of milk. Do not return.

They will fear your four-legged
crawl, your wild grumbling that
sounds just faintly like
a human name.

Losing Ground

Untangle my knots,
this echo tunnel,
this dead battery.

Untidy life, barge
leaking oil, dolphin
thrashing a tuna net.

Useless life, wharf
with no docks, phone
ripped from the wall.

How young we were,
the smallest twinge
of love enough reason.

Gaps I cannot leap,
fresh dread, lanterns
floating in the lilacs.

Therianthropy

In your absence, I am animal: no sense of time, each puddle a sea,
each piece of cinder a swarm of bees. I masquerade as human,
spinning strands of hair into gold.

The villagers march to prepare for your return, but until I touch
your face, the holes on the surface of the moon seem closer.
I breathe my own atmosphere of crisis:

stuttered heart, crashing temperature. Having traversed
worlds and miles in the static of my own worry, I am nowhere,
sniffing the air for your scent.

Self-Portrait as Naturalist

Bright angel of the circling wolves, bless
their tongues, their teeth sharp as harpoons.

Do not shame them for their hunger, their
zodiac moods, the children they steal to raise,

feral, happy, birth names erased to grunting,
faces stained with blackberries, hands chafed

to blisters, howls turned hymns in their mouths.
Missing daughters with thin wrists run wild

in the thickets, break twigs and branches,
palms in the dirt, the woods heavy with

their sweet breath. Aspen leaves rustle silver
as the sea, anthems rising from the shadows.

Bless them all, the oil in their thick coats,
their seasonless loyalty, my reasonless fear.

Provisions

Before we separated,
we buried a stash
of weapons, set them
deep in this meadow,
a faint trickle of birdsong
easing our labor.

Now there is only
a charred field of holes.
I charge the valley like
a horse ridden rough—
wild, ragged, and praying
for death.

Two AM, Waning

I have swallowed a passel
of tacks along my thick tongue.
Clocks tick. Time bends. The river
outlines the crooked coast of a smile.
Not mine. Whose I cannot say.
The tacks click against the backs
of my teeth. Only the moon
can discern my Morse code.

*

Now the moon wears a wire.
It needs to know my secrets. It has
bound me to itself with wire, skin
rubbed red. I try to hide, but there it is
with its light. I leap from a cliff and
hope it will catch on a ledge. The wire
snaps. The river laughs. I plummet
in the moonless dark.

*

Now my legs are broken. Buzzards
circle over me. The moon is herded
into a van and kidnapped. The river
is dry. I am alone. It is what I wanted.
But now I don't want it. This is always
the way with me. The moon probably
feels the same. Or not. It probably
finds me ridiculous.

*

Now I want the river to wash me
away. I hunch in the shrill of my own
thinking. My legs are healed, but fear
knots my esophagus. The sheets here
are thin, and I throw them over the sill
to escape. My hands lose grip and slip

outlaw into the air. The moon has no
hands to catch me.

After the Fires
(a nightmare)

Sparrows enter through doors and windows, lured
by unseen forces, exit in a flurry of chimney smoke.

Stain of flutter. Shimmering carcinogens. Not burning
but batting wings to ash. To ashes. Not burnt but

spurting from the funnel smudged and frenzied, some
dark thing possessing them. Passing through the stack,

they emerge changed and skittering. This is the reason
I shake in doorways, cringe at hinges, tremble when

I am drawn toward some sunrise, some small
kindness, anything tender. Pressure in my chest,

a column building—a plume of sparrows rises.

I Remember You Best

on summer afternoons—the flintseed
light, chimes that shiver but don't quite

ring. The dross and the laundry done, the startled
sob of waking already hours away, I watch the neighbors burn

branches downed by last night's storm. Cinders cluster
like mayflies then sizzle, short-lived, in the damp grass.

As dusk approaches, I ignite
torches against the sting. Inside,

the winter coats, pockets loaded with ice, laugh
at my sundress, its straps and froth fleeting.

You hate the cold. Outside, the yard percusses
with birdsong, subtle instrument hammering

memory to my backbone. The wind
can only sputter, my breath a caul

in the humid air. Night's guillotine offers
no quick misery. It lowers its blade all too slow.

Logging the Loss

I find out on a Tuesday. I find out on the phone and hide my face, contorted into shapes grotesque and try hard not to look like crying. The phone's pink rubber case clings to my cheek like a slug, the words crawling slow into my ear. Breathing becomes a mystery, my how-to manual written in Portuguese. This room is too small to contain the news. Trees engrave your initials in their trunks, your name painted in the muted blush of dusk.

After a week, my waffles taste like cardboard, and the television is a blur. Having deciphered the basics of the manual, I can move the breath in and out. Inspire e expire. I go to work, but have no memory of what I've done when it is time to leave. I heat up a Lean Cuisine French bread pizza, my culinary skills forgotten, and watch a documentary about mountain gorillas. Your name guides them to the sweet leaves they chew in stoic silence.

Sometimes you whisper in my ear, mostly when I am outside hiking with the dog (who used to bite your ankles). It's not the wind, not my imagination. I would know your voice anywhere, and no one else ever called me baby—if anyone else ever does, I will rip out his throat and leave him here to rot with the fallen trees. This forest echoes each syllable of you, your soft sibilants, your fricatives slick as machetes in the underbrush.

I can go months and not miss you, then a bowl of guacamole will break me. I carry dark glasses and tissues everywhere. I spend more and more time outside, listening for you in the hiss of traffic, seeking your rumble of end stops that will bring the mountains low. But you are gone, and nothing brings you back. Even in winter, I walk for miles, your name a mist in my mouth.

What I Do in August

You were once as much a part of me
as blood, a new kind of cell. Now
I search for you everywhere—
at the dilapidated silo, at the bottom

of a single-malt. Behind the church,
they have repaved Main Street, painted
new crosswalks to give me boundaries.
Still, on each warm night, I wander until

I arrive at our old house, pull your book
from my jacket, find you in each space.
You are a mark that will not wash from
my skin, a hush rustling inside my skull.

Lost Birds

My temperature spikes untamed and alien, a wheel of sweat with each fevered reach at sleep. The bathroom beckons with its cold tiles. But I had forgotten your robe still nested on its hook, the talons of your broken comb.

A still life of lost intimacies.

I fill up the sink to float my hands, cracked and curled to claw with trembling. The glass block window permits a haze of shimmering half-light, offers a view of three eggs hatching in nearby branches. I arrange an altar on the shower ledge – slivers of pink soap, bobby pins, your hair pulled from the drain.

I worship for hours, all disarrayed devotion.

One fledgling falls from the nest and snaps me lucid, sends me outside to stoop and hoist the barely-feathered wreck back home. I have heard how mothers reject their offspring if handled by human hands, but I am no longer human. The mother bends to preen and feed it welcome.

This is something like a second chance, something like mercy on the animal I am.

The Alphabet of Indecision

There is no easy way to say it. Words are useless, though there are so many. Cantaloupe. Armageddon. Undulating. I sort through the thesaurus to look for some assistance: Blight. Catastrophe. Disaster. Eruption. Fiasco. This will take a long time.

I call you and say, "Where are you? I need you." You have no reply. The words flop and prattle their way around my tongue and make no sense. I am not ready. I am crying, and you do not respond. You are an asshole. A bastard. A cocksucker. A dick. I have no trouble choosing these words.

I wade through piles of reference books, text circling my ankles like prison tattoos. Grief. Holocaust. Inferno. Jailbreak. Killshot. Letdown. None of these are accurate; they are blurry, imprecise, lack proper weight. I need a word that settles like a shot put in my palm, one that needs to be spun and thrust, not just tossed.

I call you and say, "Where are you? Answer me, damn it." You try to answer but can't. My hands are empty; I deserve more than this. You are a motherfucker. A ne'er-do-well. An oaf. A prick. You can't help but be a little jealous.

I fill spiral notebooks with options: Quake. Rockslide. Sucker-punch. Tsunami. I research other languages to see if any words will resonate, but most of it is untranslatable. I should create a word for what this is. Perhaps I should create a whole language, a number system, a mountain of hieroglyphs. It might take less time.

I call you and say, "Where are you? Where the fuck are you?" Your silence is a hammer, a nail, a dart, a knife. I call you useless. A vacuum. Worthless. They are not the right words, but they are something. They are xylophones ringing amidst tubas. They are yellow fireflies in a vast black sky. They are zephyrs when they should be hurricanes. They are all I have for you.

I Dream of Waking

Muscles stretched tight
over
bones, I know this is
the end,
birds soaring from envelopes,
dropping
the alphabet like seeds
into dirt
where serpents, cold tongues
forked
and roaring, shed summer skins,

where a man
stands rooted to the banks
of a river,
the sun making shadows of his arms,
while
I pulse the dark with bright
ruin,
call all the lost on their scraped
knees
to sing with me in rough-hewn
harmony,

spinning a hum to plague the air
above
the lake, to catch my sails,
to drag

me like an anchor toward
a future
I cannot see.

Matins with Horses and Light

Called from the stall of morning,
light gallops toward the gate—no,

it doesn't. It arrives in the regular
way, the earth spinning oblivious

in its own rhythm. If light could be
a horse, it would not gallop, anyway.

From what I know of light, a gallop
would be much too bold. And though

we have manufactured light, captured
it in wires and filaments, we cannot

yet hold the sun, cannot rein its burning,
lasso or tackle it into submission.

Let me start again: called from the stall
of morning, I rise and stumble to the gate.

I am not light. I do not gallop. I am ash
and shadow, huddled in the hay,

waiting to be saddled, waiting for
the bit to copper my soft tongue.

A Case for Gravity

I arrived just as flames billowed
and firemen barred the doors.

A sudden whoosh and thud.
Body, I could tell you. Jumper.

Eyes closed, I shunned
the certain wreckage.

But there was no body.
This was a night for the living,

the thud a duffle of photographs.
My eyes widened to moons

as the firemen laddered their way
toward small white hands flashing

in the smoke like stars. I could tell
you that they saved her. I could say

this is a metaphor for pessimism
or hope, that it was me up there

trying to save the past, dreading
the free fall. I could tell you that

they saved me, but that would be
a lie. I'm still at the window, waiting

for someone to spot my pale limbs
flailing in the dark.

Trigger

Through the bedroom window, a burst of cloud
and setting sun hovers like the aftermath
of some silent bomb, its destructive path
slow and spreading over hours, a shroud,
much how a forgotten memory waits
in your veins until a sudden spark explodes
it back into life, a shotgun that loads
itself, and you can't help but excavate
the gore, dig around for shrapnel to pluck
as cure, as if a thought could be removed,
which you know is impossible, yet unproven,
so you try to tie it off—holy fuck,
the bleeding—and you know you cannot die
from memories, but the pressure on your skin
seems safe, so you pull tighter and begin
to feel a better pain, at least a kind
you understand—and god, there's still that light
at the window, that fiery ball of light.

Part Three: We Feast on This Believing

Day One Again

The sky is halfway scarlet —
dawn or dusk, I cannot tell.
I am cold but will not build a fire.
I tried earlier, but even
the embers glowed too bright
for my selfish quarantine,
my limbs and brain in a mutual
march toward oblivion. I compose
letters to my longing—dearest
raw meat, dearest lush—
and outside the river accuses.
I try to pray, my anguished knees
stuccoed with carpet burns.
The folds in the blinds
show me slices of stars.
I clasp my hands together
and gasp as you return
and touch my face, my flesh
alive, remembering itself
as a person, as a body
in the world.

In the Garden

A convent of branches offers cloistered
shade, a blessing for our sunburned skin,
birds exhausting their arias as day exits.

Wind shivers the leaves, plush moss
beneath us, the sky rehung with stars,
washed with hymns and singing.

Your touch sparks me to simmer—peonies
nod their heads. They know this immaculate
burning, their insides flaming with ants.

Since Nightmares are a Kind of Dreaming

You cry out and I cradle your head. I cradle it in my arms and make you look at me. You lash out, and I make you look at me. The universe unravels, your irises blue and washed with oceans and nebulas. Your eyes brim, and I stare, trace your cheek, your jaw, with my fingertips. I trace your soft skin, your hard angles of bone. Fragile, sugar-spun. How easily I could twist and break you.

You shiver and flail, in need of anchoring. I moor and settle you. The universe unravels, and I fall through you, into you. I crawl inside your ribcage and curl into a ball. I crawl inside you, and my weight holds you to the world, to this bed, and you cannot leave it. No matter how loud you cry out. I will tether you, anchor you. I will cradle you, even when the bough breaks. Even now that it is breaking.

Salvage

We pick through the rubble under the pier:
a tangled net, a towline, an amber
bottle half-buried in silt and seaweed.
All can be of use: the line to pull clear

of quicksand, the net for trapping
minnows, the glass as tool or weapon.
You present a bouquet of reeds gathered
with a bow of old balloons, flourish it

with a grin. In these circumstances,
it will suffice. Your eyes a mansion.
This raft a ferry. Some small god dances
at the window, ticking off all our sins.

Starting Over

We scribe our skins with
flowers, steal water from
birdbaths for our strange
ablutions, our fragile frames
steeled against loneliness.

We draw and pair each single
sock from the dryer, all secrets
stored away to share as stories
in our old age. We pluck new
shoots from damp meadows,

shine coating our throats.
Steam rises, soaks our sleeves
with mist, a sweet and welcome
chill. Inside, a kettle whistles
summer, summer, summer.

Finally, An Understanding of Scale

The flight delayed. The package
late. The radiator broken, smoking.
The bread that will not rise.

A straying lover, the salty
screaming. Old vows shredded.
Night of one relentless cry.

Separation. A foreign singularity.
The house empty, echoing.
A stuttering shuffle to get by.

The weeks apart. The scab and split
of mending. The heart raw, fetid.
Time's slow-tortured tick a crime.

None of this was tragedy, although
I deemed it so, my pity headed
inward to feed a selfish need to pine.

This Being the Usual Signal

Every morning, nausea snakes my throat.
Evening no better. Despite your insistence
on my rest, a new world requires all hands.

My fevered face welcomes breeze, sweat
drying as the moon rises over the loess hills.
Your touch on my neck, feathers and silk.

We lie together, teeter on sleep, float between
the now and the before, push down the old
fears. When we wake, we walk to the river,

choose the smoothest stones for our ritual,
each one a dream we cradle then skip, rolling
the names of the lost just under our tongues.

We are painting the bedroom

dark, the better for sleeping, brown like my eyes, you said, (may we all find that one person who will compare our eyes to Ralph Lauren paint colors instead of noticing the chipped polish on our left foot) but my eyes aren't brown at all, and this mistake could indicate catastrophe but since you cannot tell the difference between the blue chair and the black chair, you are easily forgiven, especially since you also cannot seem to see the skin as it sags on my aging neck, compelling me to lift my chin always to the sky where, you can't see it, but all the planets in our solar system could fit between here and the moon, the moon that men have walked upon, the moon we can almost reach out and touch on nights like this when it is full and we have finished painting, that moon with its face staring down at us through the window, (may we all find that one person who will pretend time isn't changing us, that we are still beautiful) the moon winking just beyond our fingertips.

Back to Music

The wind is a tin rattle against
ramshackle windows, the sills
stuffed with paper to tame its bite.

We paint stars on the rough ceiling,
an exhibit of wishes unchanged by day.

I sneak one leg out from under
our quilt of scraps and rags, clutch
the tarnished locket at my throat.

You run your hand across my ribs
like a harpist, each key change closer

to crescendo, then whisper my name
to build a bridge from burn to wonder.
An engine's revving breaks the stillness,

then birdsong. Then an inhaled rest note
as you bend to pluck another string.

Continuing

So then, the old telling of stories:
birds migrating across rushes,
fledglings nested in forsythia.

So then, the old wringing of hands:
wooden bridge missing three slats,
glaciers breaking into fjords.

So many reasons for not believing,
rocket fire webbing the sky in places
whose names the news cannot pronounce.

So our story is the best story
and look, there are tracers
scribing our names in the dark.

Redux

When we met again, I noticed
something in the air—exhaust
or exhumation, a little hint
of rot beneath the sweet.

This is a truth we can believe—
every paired and mended thing
changes its form. The binding
of hands loosens to slipknot.

Each day we wake and test
the stitches, darn the tears.
We thread our limbs, lace
our fingers. We hang on.

Acknowledgments

Thank you to the following journals that graciously published these poems, some in different forms:

Apple Valley Review: "Bringing in the Sheaves"
The Boiler Journal: "Lost Birds"
Cease, Cows: "Strut and Fret"
Connotation Press: "Preamble," "The Wind Lulled and It Commenced Raining," "I Put False Hope in Celestial Bodies"
The Dialogist: "After the Fires"
DMQ Review: "First Night Alone"
Escape into Life: "Continuing"
Extract(s): "The Alphabet of Indecision"
Heron Tree: "Surviving a Midwestern Winter"
Kettle Blue Review: "What I Do in August," "This Being the Usual Signal"
The Lableletter: "The Attraction of Opposites"
Oyez Review: "Compline with Folded Arms"
Pirene's Fountain: "Provisions"
Pretty Owl Poetry: "I Remember You Best"
Redactions: "Before and After"
Stone Highway Review: "Split"
Sou'wester: "Traveling Draws the Veil"
Sugar House Review: "Matins with Horses and Light"
Sugared Water: "Self-Portrait as Naturalist"
Wherewithal: "Day One," "A Litany of Sorrows"
White Stag: "I Swear I Am Not Your Ahab"

The poem "Before and After" consists primarily of found images from The Journals of Lewis and Clark, edited by Bernard DeVoto (Mariner 1997). Poem titles with asterisks are quotes from the same source material.

About the Author

Donna Vorreyer lives and writes in the Chicago area where she is a veteran middle school teacher. Her poetry and prose have appeared in many journals and anthologies and have been nominated for both Pushcart and Best of the Net awards. She is the author of a previous collection with Sundress (*A House of Many Windows*) and seven chapbooks, most recently *Encantado*, a collaboration with artist Matt Kish (Red Bird Chapbooks, 2015).

Praise for *A House of Many Windows*

"The poems that comprise this enviable collection are unflinching and fearless, crafting new definitions for the definition of woman—as mother, as lover, as flawed and singular being. Donna Vorreyer has written these revelatory verses from the caverns of her own body—her commitment to the breath of each stanza is formidable. And that's why this book is unforgettable."

—Patricia Smith

"Vorreyer writes, 'Who cares if the night is blind / its white eye plucked and hooded?' yet these brave, sometimes elegiac poems are about caring, about how one goes on even when the weight of intense feeling is crippling. Desire, loss, the humble and glorious body, the great subjects of what it means to be human are deftly exfoliated in these poems of disassemblage and re-creation."

—Laura McCullough

"'I have a need to carry things,' says the speaker in Donna Vorreyer's A House of Many Windows, a Millay-like sequence on longing—not for a lover, but for a child she can't have. Fiercely, she enlists poetry to conceive her tie to the unborn—'My uncoupled sonnet, my comma / splice. Forgive the mediocre world, / ill-versed in our intimate literacy'—and to the boy she will eventually adopt and raise. Such mysterious and steadfast love makes Vorreyer's poems part of a wider narrative, having to do with human connection at its core—as something way, way thicker than blood."

—Douglas Goetsch

Other Sundress Publications Titles

What Will Keep Us Alive, Kristin LaTour
ISBN 978-1-939675-25-5 | | $14.00

Ha Ha Ha Thump, Amorak Huey
ISBN 978-1-939675-23-1 | | $14.00

Stationed Near the Gateway, Margaret Bashaar
ISBN 978-1-939675-20-0 | | $14.00

Till the Tide: An Anthology of Mermaid Poetry, Ed. Trista Edwards
ISBN 978-1-939675-14-9 | | $18.00

Exodus in X Minor, Fox Frazier-Foley
ISBN 978-1-939675-18-7 | | $10.00

Confluence, Sandra Marchetti
ISBN 978-1-939675-16-3 | | $14.00

major characters in minor films, Kristy Bowen
ISBN 978-1-939675-19-4 | | $14.00

Fortress, Kristina Marie Darling
ISBN 978-1-939675-13-2 | | $14.00

Hallelujah for the Ghosties, Melanie Jordan
ISBN 978-1-939675-15-6 | | $14.00

Not Somewhere Else But Here: A Contemporary Anthology of Women and Place,
Eds. Erin Elizabeth Smith, T.A. Noonan, Rhonda Lott, and Beth Couture
ISBN 978-1-939675-11-8 | | $20.00

When I Wake It Will Be Forever, Virginia Smith Rice
ISBN 978-1-939675-10-1 | | $14.00

The Lost Animals, David Cazden
ISBN 978-1-939675-07-1 | | $14.00

A House of Many Windows, Donna Vorreyer
ISBN 978-1939675-05-7 | | $14.00

The Hardship Post, Jehanne Dubrow
ISBN 978-1-939675-03-3 || $14.00

Too Animal, Not Enough Machine, Christine Jessica Margaret Reilly
ISBN 978-1-939675-02-6 || $10.00

Gathered: Contemporary Quaker Poets, Ed. Nick McRae
ISBN 978-1939675-01-9 || $15

The Old Cities, Marcel Brouwers
ISBN 0-9723224-9-3 || $14.00

One Perfect Bird, Letitia Trent
ISBN 0-9723224-8-5 || $14.00

Like a Fish, Daniel Crocker
ISBN 0-9723224-7-7 || $14.00

The Bone Folders, T.A. Noonan
ISBN 0-9723224-6-9 || $14.00

Especially the Deer, Tyurina Allen, Mary Beth Magin, and Julie Ruble
ISBN 0-9723224-0-X || $12.95